PROPOSITIONS and PRAYERS

PRO
POSI
TIONS &
PRAYERS
LISE
DOWNE

Book*hug Press
Toronto

Library and Archives Canada Cataloguing in Publication

Title: Propositions and prayers / Lise Downe.
Names: Downe, Lise, author.
Description: Poems.
Identifiers: Canadiana (print) 2020029489x | Canadiana (ebook) 20200294946
    ISBN 9781771666374 (softcover) | ISBN 9781771666381 (EPUB)
    ISBN 9781771666398 | ISBN 9781771666404 (Kindle)
Classification: LCC PS8557.O829 P76 2020 | DDC C811/.54—dc23

Printed in Canada

The production of this book was made possible through the generous
assistance of the Canada Council for the Arts and the Ontario Arts Council.
Book*hug Press also acknowledges the support of the Government of
Canada through the Canada Book Fund and the Government of Ontario
through the Ontario Book Publishing Tax Credit and the Ontario Book Fund.

Book*hug Press acknowledges that the land on which we operate is
the traditional territory of many nations, including the Mississaugas
of the Credit, the Anishnabeg, the Chippewa, the Haudenosaunee
and the Wendat peoples. We recognize the enduring presence of many
diverse First Nations, Inuit and Métis peoples, and we are grateful for
the opportunity to work on this land.

For my brother Bill.

PROPOSITIONS

a crack competes with the window
with a view of nighttime plus the loose ends
and colourful scholars, pastoral landscapes
tumbling forward and back
an improvisation of skies, something wistful
crescendos, the probability of a pause
meticulous groupings, traffic
trademarks adjacent to plastic tubes
it can only happen to countless objects
composition, courage
winded on water

dried flowers powdered in the atrium
the firmament and the weather it holds enveloping
the slow growth forest
in broad daylight a tornado, centrifugal palette of violent
ultraviolet, dark blue in dark blue
voltage returning to the unyielding rock
blasting the loosened soil, fresh surfaces
each rumble a remnant already fading
parameters a delicate whorl
on the mound cocktails with a pair of tall pitchers
walking the walk off, a tangent reconciled

as chance would have it, thrushes
a hush among the hard-to-find
little dwellings enter the unsuspecting mind
dressed-up animals, lofty authoritarians always
the details, gaps, invisible squares
weary a genuine article cracks
a shattering by arrows, at or intervals
adequate, but foraging

this could be the difference, and this
the way a whistle admits to reading
an obscurity of trees, a myriad
picture a goat on a steep incline
rescue and a lot getting chilled
delusion on a plateau
instruments in the course of a sentence
turned round, a single, already, cardinal
direction
ambling to and fro

for once a missing element and his right arm
overcast skies, foreboding also a language
you knew, the horizon between longing curved
a few rushes smitten but paler
one could have rowed, vanished in an instant
into velvet blouses, a wall of cities pointing to another
reference
pumpkin or elderberry
barefoot in a wash of green
its poignant pigment undone and redone
a tunnel bored, a surface interspersed
with rivulets

nothing if not rhythmic
a smattering by drilling spotted with holes
a cushion complete while whirring or rattling while
others crown and drive, singly they fledge
like orphans
sharp and shapely, like
how the mood heralds a repetition of nervous systems
hastening to add pictures as frames
along the liquid edges muttering and a protracted wall
a bowl of scarlet, a bright yellow envelope, a single note
corresponding to three days of solitude hand-marked *Urgent*
a mouthful and measure a few miles from the sea

cradled in her palm the crescent moon above
a button on a railway platform
better yet
hundreds—thousands of numinous swords
the real world pouring in this afternoon
where you are headed, rescued
from the brink of dullness
a coalition of roses and cucumbers
letting it all fall away *per se*
avoiding a conflict of punctuation
favoured by sorting
sorting

if ever a fluid sign, the water table's
sense but slipping
you, too, harbour reasons to believe
nonetheless, quickening in response to the vast
frame of reference, *I want to wait*
you said the crashing waves
configure an intricate choreography
unpredictable beauty with what remains
arrives
washed up on a red sea's shores, hypnotic
evocative processions

barges moored in the canal, ambient music
piped into nightfall once the fireworks begin
irregular wakes collide, booming inside
a plausible scenario
surely there's someone to blame
or sue
surely no law is more essential than
summer and a bay of constables, a lot of downed trees
let's
train our eyes to look hard
lean in closer, into my spoon
leftovers on the window seat, leftovers
and several grains of sand

after the asteroid, tiny red seed beads
but not for long, think faded photographs
now they're settled, ignore flattery
the billowing pantaloons
agreed, there *is* a blur about them
open walkways cascade from every surface
past squatting, past terror, past the expansive
ancient stone emerging like the sun through fog
it's a long way back to the parking lot
miniature orange trees blossoming on the third floor
star-studded and improbably narrow
too rich and I'd wager too thin

perfectly good reason to believe it's all routine
and unremarkable
the back door and tiny patio
these are the givens mid-morning alludes to
reading like a primer of guiding principles with you, right now
keep cool
keep the weekend
the sun-warmed laneway, the word cloud
constellating above it
an electric fan whirs in the background
its rhythmic accompaniment conjuring
up another secular space

no whoops or catcalls, just the deep silence of indigo walls
a focus inward on an unhappy neighbour
who could be anybody, the biggest mistake of your life
methodical, monastic, schlepping up the ramp
an order of ascending mass
victory, in the end, blows the banner down
everyone and afterward hard to swallow
incongruent yet plausible
as simple as flip-flops
worn year-round, one hand over
the other hand under

prophetically it vanishes, the only candidate
trusted with water
I'm busted and much uglier than anyone I've ever seen
this poverty of wrinkled suits
June of 1961, which doesn't make it any easier
rehearsed old grievances and suddenly
the word *hearse*, a Cinderella story of
gold-nibbed fountain pens and inkwells
the vacated apartment giving the remaining day
a languid *Hi*
plus a few empathetic words, in fact, a heartfelt speech

what entering would entail
we and they recognize whose doors swing freely
in and out, private jokes
and the raw fact of discovery make it urgent, vivid
dependent on the red wheelbarrow
especially since it was almost pitch-black, nonetheless
we filled in the darkness
recollections of a human life, after all
so I'm standing in front of the door
really ticked off, thinking

white lost in blue, could have
should have known someone would keep
on motioning to follow, stepping forward
into a propeller of clenched fists, the opacity of white
wooden tables, signs above the booth, a fraction
no paper to show for the medals where a lectern waited
it, too, wanting to break away
beginning with catalpa
farewell my heiress, my fortune

tremendous happiness of watching part of what's
taken as normal, delphiniums in the back
foretelling an obsession with codes, mysterious scars
thinner and thinner slices, the room
with multiple views
not everyone appreciating candour
the endless spiralling banister, flickers on the lawn
blue jays in the blue spruce, magic in the meadow
can muster, hearken to me now

confusing, the hand a rail
one of which of two is subtlest, the difference
betwixt an opening or valves
the man on the street on the street
the ruins, one's every move scripted
a kick in the shins, a raft
or an impossibly tiny basement doomed
from start to finish
however, if you recall
the main impediment cropping up at the outset
hands dry, lips moving
no real guidance
still
grateful to have been there

but never mind, once the foraging begins
depending on how
with practically no time at all
you look and
the little becomes obvious, the breeze
barely audible, close to hand
vague stirrings undetectable
but wait
we must, unearthly gospel
walls crammed full of cones
a tablecloth, the now cracked glass
and all the irreplaceable stuff in here

quoted as saying no surprise
perhaps
or if they're nervy, emulating a fresco
the enigma of its composition begins
to crumble, foreshadowing our civilization
everyone fails, craves an audience
the neon marquee—a voice from the road
keeps casting around, starved for attention
the whistling of arrows sure to make
sure you're listening

a blanket of cornflowers in the wake of melting snow
one shade blends into the other
vaulting to the next installment, trust
in that voodoo you do, loosening
what is already obviously
a license to invent, the curious prospect of clarity
repeated as a refrain one is told to walk
a certain distance in a certain direction, close
to the place to what end, ready to roll down
the revelations follow
and *This?* we ask
and she answers
Absolutely

the climate moist and extremely old, animals
again, mingling among animal spirits
trusted by both the chance encounters
a sustained ovation clear and inclined
to keep the debate going in dots and dashes
a single unifying argument willing to work the crowd
one must stand empty
left with part of the pleasure, utterly spent
overhearing
everyone's got a story, pal

a periodic handful of pages
plural, always plural and
pure fascination, transforming
vocals to vapour to portals
rehearsals "adhere and appear like ghosts"
a little before midnight an owl
a consolation of roses, the lake's still surface
I wonder is it possible, can we hope
to be reasonably comfortable
having lost even our bearings, those fleeting revelations

whether visionary or visible, we recall
the names, the ether as it drifted across
the shallows
leading to miracles on all sides
to why you're here, this day
attending the guardian figures
who never really went away, they
knew all about the notions beginning to flow
the catastrophic flooding
baffled only by the "is, was not, is not, was"
and an uncanny clicking
sound

we're dealing with a vast and vital
resonance, a commonwealth coexistent
with strangeness you never know what ought to figure
prominently and, I mean
not knowing, in fact, but willing to reconsider
a force field, a compass disoriented
and kindness followed by compassion and
what, exactly, is bent when assigned to change
what singular what history what while attending

elder, sentinel, sage
the seed may have travelled vibrant pink
on a gust of wind, it is chance
eluding us thus until the fifth day
when a blueprint gradually materializes
fade-out of a single sorrow and a puzzle of palm trees
a Mediterranean profile on a nearby windowsill
sunlight falls on them
naturally
in advance of the beach and dune, the shady quadrangle
the sound sleep needed after the beautiful and
   undesirable elements
unfurl or vanish

not like those other guys
for whom the books, bells and whistles told
or were intended
whose wit and willingness hold
fast to parts familiar or unfathomed—who cares?
we're pretty sure to find a clue quickly
in this cavernous space
the lawn and grounds difficult to predict
the way the clock, catching sight of its hands
settles into a rhythm of *ready or not*
eons manifest as a single vine embracing a ruin
unperturbed
a mile long, a mile wide and a mile deep

drown down the whisper of meaningful arrangements
dispatch letters and cables
the question of time and measurement
and an incredible eye
weeks of labouring, broad strokes
and a playing card the size of
think offhand of
a prop, not
a conventional photovoltaic panel
forever dependent on the light
that spans, empties and fills
and when it frays is self-repairing

sounds right

euphoniously named blinds—I mean drapes
can't divulge
much
this ear practically giddy
the look of a naked eye on a treasure map
seven days running into the field
the earth between two circular stones
size the moon above my head
not not an echo
or example of how the rings widen
but all, all
most

this because we remember
the waterfall and protruding rock ledges
a long, low line of hedges
the sun in silence
miracles
need no coaxing, only us
left in silence
see-sawing and gradually ascending

formulas guide their pencils through
dry roots down
to the present, the fourth century
dazed in the aftermath, foliated
colouring the historic divide
hard to know where to start, chips of rock keep flying
and yet we feel
no pain
like it or not
one false step could be an opening into a room
never seen before with blank, almond-shaped eyes
reminiscent of ancestors, illustrations to follow

scores of doors on a small scale scattered wide
and relatively empty space, the pines
tossed against the sky
saving as grace falls free of the wall
so many moving parts the number of breaths
and the man behind the curtain
the furnishings speak for themselves, their origins
an unmistakable cadence blowing
blue within blue, blue to play again with blues
in several or a dozen different languages
let's say boughs or beams
all after quiet after all
all upward always indefinitely

memorials in the sand, still blank contours
where renderings belong and take off
again—like a shot—at an unearthly hour
mud trickles with unfulfilled ambition
I...I'm glad to see you too, you've remained
transcendently goofy, smooth and well rounded
calm even when confronted with the prospect of here
being also and always
an elsewhere, as is your habit
a hangover from infancy singing at all hours
and crocuses, not scissors, to ease the pain
Sunday in Santiago resplendent even in grey

what lingers after the pomp
the puerile, the unfair and galling
when all is finally cradled in the shade of sycamore
sheltered from the fire and kettles
irregular grades and surfaces
the rabbit—and the little foot that walked into its heart
return to scratch and scatter the opened field
could it really be
the coming of ground coming to light so
click

Gone.

and yet one hears
laughter from the theatre, rainfall
then a period of awkwardness, pretend
a dead bird *is* the present, rocks and sandy soil
in the mezzanine such flair and fury
no memory of how the bruises got there
the top of the escalator, stage and footpaths
confound us, the right angles
half within and half outside
the locomotive in the front foyer
discombobulated, inexhaustible
world

it's conceivable, at least, when
thus assembled, what stands out
are the slight and irregular, fields of their own
elegant in a wealth of shadows, distinguishing spades
from spades the boos and whistles
(there in the shadows)
puzzling how they languished
mute, but even more
the incongruous hint circulating
unhindered
not in the mist but the stoniest walls
first stations in a long tangle of strings
improvise and threaten
the fabric
of things

the last episode by analogy
and certainly before proceeding we'll note
the irregular placement
added like an afterthought
the core and never thinking
much of it, loosening greenish-yellow
from yellowish-green, the fish from the flame to be sure
ghostly whiteness bearing witness, we don't understand exactly
what
it is, but billboards are—no matter
what
definitely no accident

it could have been, is almost, an ally
which it wasn't, of course, but a step
camouflaged as a niche
leaving us free, you see, ear-deep in watermelon
thigh-high on the crumbling garden wall
flashlights on
fragments of the colossal head and hand
swirls of cotton candy by the fountain
the fountain is escaping no one has realized!
abandoning the fortress, yes, even the factories

into the concave, now convex, no concave
impact of fumbling efforts, the visitor lingers
long slanting lines and deep relief, and
incidental reflection adding twigs to log houses
the octagon holds it all together, addresses
the congregation ignoring the flying buttress
increasingly heavy beads of sweat
deeper recesses of the folding screen
swing alongside the liturgical reading
yellow, green, blue, magenta
and isn't that St. George?

out here I have no treasure
I have an aversion to lunatics
I have
glossy chestnuts, a powder-blue egg
one golden leaf stem reduced to a matchstick
an alloy of comfort and strangeness, something
undivided
less scared, more intuitive, almost sacred
waters guide us further afield, beyond thought
or thinking
where the waves break into a tide pool of splendid pieces
salt spray (again) and sunburned brows
an end in and of ourselves

remarkable the wish and whim
but more extraordinary the implications
from what quarter I'll never know, nor should you
reflect, even in winter, on
what lies north of the great divide
what constitutes the conditions of fading
what mines similarity, seeks refuge
stands, face flushed, on a steep-sided hill
complex
predetermined, as plain as
day, difficult to identify why the wit and the will
get ever so weirder and weirder

imagine the relief of the lost correspondent
scarcely believing his ears or
what resembles the matador's flourish unleashing
god knows what
a bit of a mess but appealing
oddly enough, regardless of the title you call it by
after the first few pages
rules don't penetrate or apply
the editorial disappears without a trace
taking with it catastrophes we've carried
by accident, and with it a journal of twelve new rings

the broad and the bends
the heart and the end this summer
afternoons falling to the green
along with the ball wondering
what song is it going to be today?
mingled and cut through with reeds and wild guesses
a truly different feeling, the ball tender and disarming
dissolves into *terra amorphosa*
dappled darkness and
everything otherwise remains the same

without saying, or seeing
or saying it out loud
without confidence
in the pebbled ground
not knowing what to make of all the traffic
pings and trills, as far as one can tell
one must thus be lost, unsure
where the emphasis should go
at pains, so, too, the voices
the patient listeners

no matter how blue, the bluish haze
of recent memory mirrors
the horses' heads
not clatter but canter again
uncertainty long as the river
collisions, convoluted impressions
a myriad of circles, curves—a river of sparks!
and hinges prepared to spend ages
opening and closing eternally
the plot from the outset evaporates
disappearance and return
among equals

as if the portrait bleached
looked, by turns, skeptical
in thrall, sitting supine
suddenly shudders, an early warning
of more than one insufferable trait
looping back and forth
back toward why
in its provocations, the demure inward bend
and the keepsake
keep turning in time to the music
the sound tracks

wherefore the circumstantial mystery
what of charms and rattles, absorbing facts
pooled together, I mean
I'm not trying to indict anyone
but what do we know
other than quotes skirting
every margin of truth
would do anything to avoid the thatched hut
and its racy angle, the dendriform column
any thorny patch or song, and the rest
shadowing all we saw anyway
the way the light switches
anyway

a white cup and saucer, a thin wavy red line
the tenuous
but unforgettable goings-on, so
glad to see you, notions on the plus side
mountains and craters and probably
something
something *always* has to happen
the fact of a stocking for starters
not only lonely, but nylon as well
threading—not like we'd imagine
(to a cup and saucer)
but even further back, to a free-for-all
unsettling new order
or mayhem or
everything seems just fine

give me a ladder to climb on
one with high expectations
I ache seeing how easily daylight wanes
everyone walking through the door
this whole business of estuaries
words chosen, so one could say, carefully
like the last time, well, we are happy
while all the while details
on the smallest scale say
the light varies at the place where boundary knows
no limits to the messages given
easier to phrase than build

of at least *this* much we can be certain
hence the one, then two
when adding up can be taken as true
six singular numbers and perhaps
well, perhaps not
and whose tetrahedral flag is this?
you think you have a grip, know how
to highlight even the hollows
why the house rises
alongside the sun
rising, loving the ground, upside
down, bright as they say the day

could be part of the movement
misunderstandings double back
to begin with, a strategy of questions
a kind of revelation unintentional
uncanny paradox of the perfect age
anthems, hymns
the left arrow and the right
arrow
turning points to fall back on
this scenario, that analogy
and on the periphery those particles in the air
there to begin with

that's all, it's enough
because what's implied
becomes a vehicle, a
passage to get through
into places one doesn't belong
long enough to be believed
because the trick lies in switching
a quiet corner
for your thoughts, the footnotes silent
in a swivel chair, subtlety bathed in red
glow of an EXIT sign
visions that guide us

what it's not, not what it is
alone can bear the voyager
as if the tide simply went out
imperceptibly but steadily
it's like that all the time, fragility
an evening on your forehead as it happens
hints of the layering, changes
forged in a painful childhood
the shipwreck looking to outer space
and your arm that issues from a hole in
the ceiling

but no, not even when asked if any of it
rings a bell, the church tower's one unequivocal dong
we hear as concordance, taken on faith
and laughter a contrast to the frown and furrow
glimmer of the flashback staring in
rapture a series of perfect squares
considering acts of humility along the way
the spectacular is the exception, we decipher
the first line
a million light-years and lives of the in-between
the hoopla wide-eyed, never faltering

as foretold among others
on a windswept night or beach
a reservoir in figures we meet pairs and trios
there's no secret, no coincidence
but the same persistent question, the what or
wherefore, sympathies and seasons, their
coming and going a torchlight procession
why now the strangled throb
why not the mess my novel
my
what more can one ask

What's changed?

hightailing it down a Venetian alleyway
across countless bridges, schemers and dreamers
it's one glimpse of bliss after another, the deluge
the appointed hour unveiling a bronze
the sun out, briefly
candlesticks in a marble corridor
offerings of flowers or fruit it's hard to say
exactly what all the preparations are
underway, there are so many
but the blueness is unmistakable
and what about those smiles that make it sing

they said yes, with uncharacteristic forwardness
while we lingered, as if this wasn't enough
or for
given there was the warm lighting and the
animated telescope that realigned the crater
still up to its old orbits, habits, tricks
scanning the skies your destiny, your face
amid the general buzz and hummmm one could say
a likeness (a likeness) between them and
around them—look!—gold stars
and space

and sunlight on the slates and the privileged hours
after the anxieties of night
deeper shade of a remarkably calm and generous
show of hands achieving
a tranquil mind
as in "eating lunch, not *being* lunch"
everything in its place
for every good reason call it virtue amid the frenzy
not
what is wont but what can
in the most nonchalant way possible
battle an instinct to turn (turning) and run

giving thanks, in part, to the pirates
the invisible wilderness beckoning, not knowing
where we had cast ourselves
what sought translation, details
of the vision we had
a picture book with gilded letters
keywords only casually mention places
where the valuables go, sailing past the ominous cliffs
floods of blue, flashes of red
sparkles of yellow, orange and green
a thousand pink noses, two thousand bright eyes

in the unfiltered hours and prior to arrest
in the spies and cracks, in every stripe
or spot, a given signal in the aftershock
of the first few seconds
the pretense
shuffling, scuffling
flurries and revelations cast enough light
through the smoke and mirrors a haunting visage
dropping from the sky into her lap that's
one way to receive the stunning news
a liar and crook strutting on their polished surface
honestly unworthy to marry
her for all she knows

could be a fingernail the size of
a fingernail
a deck of cards, the toss of a slipper
an undertow of comedy despairs
what's missing, what gifts do we bear
phantoms, pedestals and plinths
and what's with the mopey guy's
snow cone dampening the party mood
while all the while the balustrade
beckons

Here. I'm down here.

over yonder, down by the road, near
the gate, alongside the drizzle
and stones, a coyote and fireball tumble
adjacent to the well, reflected
pits, mounds and ramps
the pitter-patter a
permanence
one might have wished for or cared
more than we already do

her calculated instrument of expression
those shaggy black bangs nearly
to her eyebrows, her entire being
guided, lickety-split, by the virtual clock
the wall in real time
sparing her an alibi her fingers thrum
against a backdrop
even the shady brim, her hat, can't fathom
what is happening underneath, naturally
we're surprised, having heard it all before
only lighter and snappier

not minding the cat, the fray
the fact the whole time it's
tied to the rising and setting of certain stars
the art of screwing up a lot wanting
credit where no claim can be made
innocent, angelic fantasy before the blizzard of feathers
enhanced the air, bewilderment
shock, sweat and peril
praying for rescue and a little altitude
but the key (the key) was
already in
by then

following the previous night's zero
the bridge concerned mainly with ritual
the underlying forces flowing beneath it
the chase, the drift, the tower remains
sleepwalking on a midnight trail
veneration of an accidentally broken plate
fragments of the spell bound
to be found, wanting

on the horizon snuff bottles
made of glass, porcelain and amber
the boulevards leading
back to the sidewalk where we stand
isn't a movie, but
if one needs cheering up
take a detour round the back
and see what's surfacing
grassland, drumlins, ocean

a spluttering candle that
seemed to come from nowhere
no one ever told me, that is
to say I never realized
what the custom was
what the signal is saying, the sun still
shining, it doesn't vary
much
these days are numberless
unlike clouds nurturing what's below
and what's above
one weeps where the water soaks in
soon, all too soon
to melt from us

this is the best
you don't exactly have to be a tuning fork
or even see one
just be nimble and direct, when you bend
down bend slowly
that way you won't arouse suspicion
don't even ask who's driving
or *Why am I doing this?*
both hands on the wheel
and so it goes, like so
on and on and soon
it is

nonetheless, limestone changes everything
thinking would be fun, to be a rare book
filched, but wait a day longer and it'll be
not fear, really, but certainly
a venue, a ponytail of voices gathering the joke
but don't mention the violence, the stained
glass window a dream standing as if in a dream
steady on, slow and steady the action unfolds
rumours of a halo, here is an image
rumours you get to decide

PRAYERS

Current Events

The day undergoes an evolution
there in the moving surfaces.
Now a landscape, now a room
what more can be made of the elevation
the backdrop and the light above.

The river you live on dispels any mob
of lingering doubt, the
gist of which says
gee, admittedly
the hours didn't pass this way earlier.

Every image underscores a corresponding
moment. It is never the same.
Yet here's one that bobs up again and again
big as apples, as brazen as
abracadabra.

The canvas exaggerates
perspective, rebellious monuments
the daily round of irregular forms.
All we've ever met on awakening
lands into look and heaven.
A calling
or cliff as it swallows our pressing concerns.

Unspent time disappears over the horizon
then comes the summons: Wake up!
revising the few hours of morning, as if
this is where the call comes from.

Prismatic moulding.
Cadences of warbler and wren.
There's no explanation.
That's simply the way it is.

The Sash of Time

Others on the terrace breathe in
the generosity of constellations
more peaceful than before, their
vast restoration swaying on tiptoe
a subtle and reassuring sign of where things stand

not exactly in the foreground, yet methodically
unfolding
an otherworldly portfolio of countless prints
outside on the terrace, too.
Would that we were so lucky

to reckon and hold her in these pages
or even an earring
or glimpse of evening, a single blade of grass
and a mood of relief that cobbles it together
softening the tremulous barriers

magnifying, unexpected and wondrous.
Would that there were more moments
a book of beginnings to propel the recurring story
a procession
like hesitations come to mind

illustrating an essential quiet
ness, or quiet
ude
alive in the lyrics, her gloves
themselves.

Little Wonder

not what advances
before

or after but
what makes room
around them

what the melody
invokes

what you think

it wants

     *

because they linger
asking

Out of all of these
how come?
Out of whose storm
and what walls?

faltering
before the entry
ways

outlying territory
and patterns

any that darken
or chart the intersection
archives of melancholy
much of the time

clear
hypnotic eyes

*

what lighting
candles
puffs of white
smoke
might signify

what break
the past
unmoors

staggered
warming
to the orange
limber
magnetic pull

*

what accident
is it
about the place

at whose nod
and with
what haste

what reigns
is surely
by the by
and far

how and
in what

masterful
but never mind
the music
nervous
and necessary

*

what one day
more or
less
recalls
one room
for the obvious
feeling

we
are after

the hero's face
the sky

before
they reckon
off and soaring

kite in the wilds
the air

downward tugs
tiny adjustments

how they exult
stringing
the dexterity
of
ducks and turns

such
slender
ness

a line
and probably a song
sparing none

here
in a way

This Might Be It

Should I find myself too captivated by a narrow fortune
now and even then intending
not to suffer
but to travel my conscience, strengthen
what might have been memory
manner and disposition, in effect

trust myself to the mercy of the lawn
lying down like we do, contemplating green
our twin faces
reflecting the sky, the canopy of trees
steadfast, sonorous
limbs that tremble.

Should I welcome
mingle and explore
all that's been emptied, drink in the distance
syllable and smooth stone
muster the palm of my hand, this lush
abbreviation gesturing to the opened spaces
running like the secret river we knew so well

running as far as we can, as far as
the concentration of pillars
pillars carved in strange figures
some white, some black, others at eye level
liberating the smell of the soil
the sneeze in the temple that sounds so echoey.

Should gentleness lead me to conceive of resilience we've known
so that, with your or some other high favour
one might be persuaded, if not by silence
then
through the chatter of confiding new voices.

Suffer me to continue no longer
but to find comfort in the tough company of rumpled shirts
and jeans, their heart-stopping way, yes, an antidote
where men and gods speak face-to-face, where
they reflect and shade
into each other.

Where we find ourselves
perhaps, borrowing from a thousand sources
isn't always or easy
it's
another article of faith sharing the footpath
where I-you-they might vault into being
up and down and eventually over.

Spooky

If not for want of mercy, we are
suddenly seamless, wandering
through unfamiliar rooms.

Guidelines becoming less and less
specific
not necessarily at odds, per se, but
a presence charges the atmosphere.

The pool is stirring.
Will it evaporate with
our differences
our uncertain bearings
as, alas
in this (involuntary)
instance

it is unnerving
to imagine
the many complicated reactions
which we (again) are
in thrall and
at pains to make plain.

Hovering like we do
like no harm was done
sentences growing longer and longer
altering an aside spoken at lunch
articulated vowels....

And how they flutter
and flee
depending on the direction you're facing.
Delicate, broken and beautiful
rippling across the gulp of seawater
descendents from a noble line dissolve—of necessity
in part of the numinous, ancestral
letter
D.

Lighten My Heart

What melts and when.
What rumour and shifty character
commemorate the fact nothing
much has changed.

No one seems to mind
the undulating trajectory of
one or another chapter.
Futility some would say

the cruelty of the times
bluer than before
in the otherwise silent room.

Nothing touches the odd hours
even an odd word.
Barely spoken of the semblance
we sense a new darkness
turning perhaps
in another century
or so
to rain.

Now all outer weather vanishes.

In the half-light there is a level
below that another
level and yet another.

Keep me from falling, failing
to step outside and greet the rain.
Help me with an opening sequence.
Allow it to skip or sidestep a thousand curses.
I'll settle for the slightest, an inkling
a double take and—whoa, it does look amazing
          lifting even
even though its pleats are bulging.

Mystery Train

It is only thus
a primeval forest of (what else?)
trees.

A stepladder fidgets
there
in the standing wood.

An invisible link
conjoins this
to that.

There are others
no one knew
knows it yet.

In its way
it's not surprising
or hard to fathom.

A sigh is never indifferent
to itself
nor a well as well.

It falls into
those who throw
an amulet in a letter.

The latter introduces
a strange new wrinkle
with bright ideas.

There lies the difference
variations
that follow.

Thereby the world is formed
tracing the finger
the sound.

      *

Meanwhile, of all
that emerges
this is the most curious.

Harking back
to the amulet, the letter
flourishes.

Amid this bounty
barely a tree
takes place.

What now?
What counts
grows leafy.

Those that rise
loftily already
take the breath away.

The long term
and getting longer
and then the idea.

Still
these nuances, like chance
ring true.

Give sway
to the rolling swell
that reverberates.

Hence the unmistakable friction
with a calmer
surface.

Ask the night
about the day's
small splashes.

How endless
the frustrations
of a shallow bath.

Coinciding with the field
the idea
of a field.

These are the poles
while all the rest
are changes.

The stakes heighten
trepidation.
Oh, what to do?

Of what does the messenger.
Of what stumbles
is how.

What, then
shifts in the margins
begins to swirl.

Why not say
you never know
what's missing.

And maybe
just maybe
it stays that way.

Dawning

And what of the clothes with no one
inside them, hung up over there where
the charm of shimmering leaves
enlivens the lull of midday.

The puzzle remains
remembering the canoe on the lake
its passage and the blue sky it came across.
Silence and syllable.
And placement.

The red canoe on the windy lake.

Flickering in the foreground and the periphery
the shorelines.
Night and the island path, lost continents
and clearings.

And they—the fisherman, painter
little water jar—where *are* they?

Bundles of twine, a network
of unsettled lines, irregular waves
no sooner surface than vanish
visible again in the morning
shining with a borrowed, cresting light.

The Same, but Different

Unfazed by the shifting tides, her passions
include water and fish
and how the eye travels between
twilight and morning.

Last summer she discovered fluid
tassels of an ancient female astronomer.
Then
her conversion was complete.

Her artifacts—their diversity—are small
quiet and intensely personal.
From the outside they are diamonds, rubies
and pearls.

Her invocations flow and flower wordlessly.
As in love, her landscapes are unframed
with slightly abstracted views, unpeopled.
On any given day the white jumps out. A dancer.
A portrait.

She inhabits the unrolling spools
unsynched church bells
and slightly crazed birds.
Holding to the light, in spite
of shadows   she has seen
beyond the cacophony
and rolls with it, them.

They all say yes
yes
of course.

As, too, do the observation decks
beginning beginning to whirl.

Acknowledgements

Earlier versions of some poems appeared in *The Capilano Review* 3.33 and 3.20, and in *Touch the Donkey* #4.

Many of the "Propositions" were published (in previous versions) as a chapbook with rob mclennan at above/ground press.

*

The phrase "adhere and appear like ghosts" is borrowed from Clark Coolidge's "Arrangement," *Talking Poetics from Naropa Institute*, July 1977.

"Blue within blue, blue to play again with blues" is a quote from Frank Lloyd Wright, *The Future of Architecture*, 1953.

*

My deepest gratitude to Sandra Ridley, and to Jay and Hazel Millar, for their kindness, engagement, and support; thanks also to the Toronto Arts Council and the Writers Reserve Program of the Ontario Arts Council for their generous assistance.

author photo: Tristan Downe-Dewdney

Lise Downe is the author of four previous collections of poetry: *A Velvet Increase of Curiosity* (1993), *The Soft Signature* (1997), *Disturbances of Progress* (2002), and *This Way* (2011). Lise also studied painting, printmaking, and jewellery design for many years. Originally from London, Ontario, Lise lives and works in Toronto.

COLOPHON

Manufactured as the first edition of
Propositions & Prayers
in the fall of 2020 by Book*hug Press

Edited for the press by Sandra Ridley
Copy edited by Stuart Ross
Type + design by Ingrid Paulson

bookhugpress.ca